The **Pebble** First Guide to

Horses

by Zachary Pitts

Consulting Editor: Gail Saunders-Smith, PhD

Capstone
press®
Mankato, Minnesota

Pebble Books are published by Capstone Press,
151 Good Counsel Drive, P.O. Box 669, Mankato, Minnesota 56002.
www.capstonepress.com

1 2 3 4 5 6 13 12 11 10 09 08

Library of Congress Cataloging-in-Publication Data
Pitts, Zachary.
    The Pebble first guide to horses / by Zachary Pitts.
    p. cm. — (Pebble books. Pebble first guides)
    Includes bibliographical references and index.
    ISBN-13: 978-1-4296-1708-6 (hardcover)
    ISBN-10: 1-4296-1708-X (hardcover)
    ISBN-13: 978-1-4296-2802-0 (softcover pbk.)
    ISBN-10: 1-4296-2802-2 (softcover pbk.)
    1. Horses — Juvenile literature. I. Title. II. Series.
SF302.P58 2009
636.1 — dc22   2008001396
Summary: A basic field guide format introduces 13 horse breeds.

About Horse Sizes

The height of a horse is measured in hands. One hand equals 4 inches (10 centimeters). Shetland ponies are measured in inches. A horse is measured from the ground to the highest point on its shoulders.

Note to Parents and Teachers

The Pebble First Guides set supports science standards related to life science. In a reference format, this book describes and illustrates 13 horse breeds. This book introduces early readers to subject-specific vocabulary words, which are defined in the Glossary section. Early readers may need assistance to read some words and to use the Table of Contents, Glossary, Read More, Internet Sites, and Index sections of the book.

Table of Contents

foal

Height:	14 to 16 hands
Weight:	1,000 to 1,200 pounds (450 to 540 kilograms)
Colors:	bay, brown, chestnut, black; has white spots
Home country:	United States
Uses:	rodeos, western riding
Facts:	• smart and calm • good with children

foals

Height: 15 to 16 hands

Weight: 1,200 to 1,500 pounds
(540 to 680 kilograms)

Colors: bay, brown, sorrel, roan

Home country: United States

Uses: rodeos, western riding, racing

Facts:
- most popular horse
- strong and quick

foal

Height: 15 to 17 hands

Weight: 1,000 to 1,200 pounds
(450 to 540 kilograms)

Colors: bay, brown, chestnut

Home country: United States

Uses: riding, driving

Facts:
- has large eyes
- smart and friendly

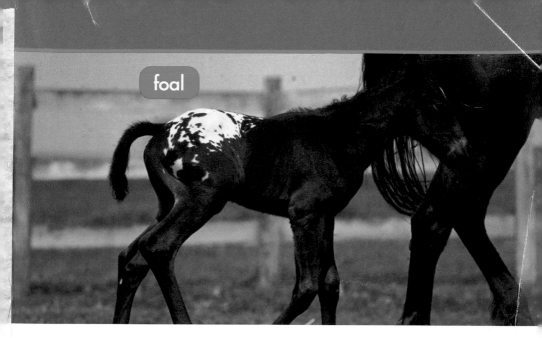

foal

Height: 14 to 16 hands

Weight: 1,000 to 1,200 pounds
(450 to 540 kilograms)

Colors: bay, chestnut, black; has spots

Home country: United States

Uses: riding

Facts:
- first used by Native Americans
- named for Palouse River in northwestern United States

foal

Height: 14 to 15 hands

Weight: 800 to 1,100 pounds
(360 to 500 kilograms)

Colors: chestnut, bay, gray, black

Home country: Saudi Arabia

Uses: riding

Facts:
- very old breed
- gentle and graceful

foal

Height:	16 to 18 hands
Weight:	1,800 to 2,000 pounds (815 to 900 kilograms)
Colors:	chestnut, sorrel, roan
Home country:	Belgium
Uses:	driving, farm work
Facts:	• able to pull heavy loads • nicknamed "gentle giant"

15

foal

Height: 16 to 18 hands

Weight: 1,600 to 1,800 pounds
          (725 to 815 kilograms)

Colors: bay, brown, black

Home country: Scotland

Uses: driving, farm work

Facts: • foot is size of dinner plate
          • hardworking and easy to train

foal

Height: 15 to 17 hands

Weight: 1,300 to 1,400 pounds
(590 to 635 kilograms)

Colors: black

Home country: Netherlands

Uses: driving, English riding

Facts: • has a thick mane and tail
• calm and willing to learn

19

foal

Height: 14 to 16 hands

Weight: 1,000 to 1,300 pounds
(450 to 590 kilograms)

Colors: gray, but darker when young

Home country: Slovenia

Uses: riding, driving

Facts:
- strong and graceful
- lives up to 35 years

foal

Height: 15 to 17 hands

Weight: 1,600 to 2,400 pounds
            (730 to 1,100 kilograms)

Colors: gray, black

Home country: France

Uses: driving, farm work

Facts: • proud and smart
            • often used in parades

23

foal

Height: 40 to 42 inches
(102 to 107 centimeters)

Weight: 300 to 450 pounds
(140 to 200 kilograms)

Colors: bay, brown, chestnut, black

Home country: Scotland

Uses: children's ponies, driving

Facts: • smart and independent
• small but very strong

foal

Height: 15 to 16 hands

Weight: 900 to 1,200 pounds
(410 to 540 kilograms)

Colors: black, bay, chestnut

Home country: United States

Uses: trail riding

Facts:
- comfortable to ride
- calm and friendly

27

foal

Height: 15 to 17 hands

Weight: 1,000 to 1,200 pounds
(450 to 540 kilograms)

Colors: brown, chestnut, gray

Home country: England

Uses: racing, riding

Facts: • smart and brave
• famous for its speed

Glossary

bay — brown with a black mane and tail

chestnut — a reddish-brown color

driving — using a harness on a horse so it can pull a cart, wagon, sleigh, plow, or carriage

English riding — a style of horseback riding based on European traditions and equipment

hand — a measurement of horse height that is equal to 4 inches (10 centimeters)

roan — sorrel, chestnut, or bay body color, sprinkled with gray or white

rodeo — a contest in which people ride horses and bulls and rope cattle

sorrel — light red body color with a lighter mane and tail color

trail riding — a type of horseback riding where riders follow marked trails

western riding — a style of horseback riding first created by Spanish and American cowboys in the western United States

Read More

Criscione, Rachel Damon. *The Quarter Horse*. The Library of Horses. New York: PowerKids Press, 2007.

Dell, Pamela. *Arabians*. Majestic Horses. Chanhassen, Minn.: A Child's World, 2007.

Internet Sites

FactHound offers a safe, fun way to find Internet sites related to this book. All of the sites on FactHound have been researched by our staff.

Here's how:

1. Visit *www.facthound.com*
2. Choose your grade level.
3. Type in this book ID **142961708X** for age-appropriate sites. You may also browse subjects by clicking on letters, or by clicking on pictures and words.
4. Click on the **Fetch It** button.

FactHound will fetch the best sites for you!

Index

Grade: 1
Early-Intervention Level: 25

Editorial Credits

Erika L. Shores, editor; Alison Thiele, designer; Jo Miller, photo researcher

Photo Credits

©2004 Mark J. Barrett, cover (Friesian), 19
Alamy/blickwinkel, 21; Mark J. Barrett, 18
Deer Creek Walkers/Mary Bittner, 27
Far Field Farm/Barbara Molland, 9
Getty Images Inc./Robert Harding World Imagery/David Tipling, 24
iStockphoto/iofoto, 15 (right); Karen Givens, cover (Arabian); Nancy Kennedy, cover (Belgian)
©Lynn Cassels-Caldwell, 23 (right)
Peter Arnold/Biosphoto/Grenet M. & Soumillard A., 23 (left); S. Stuewer, 26
Shutterstock/C. L. Triplett, 5; Condor 36, 28; Elena Elisseeva, 25 (right); Eline Spek, 10, 25 (left); Greg Randles, 4; Jeff Banke, 8; Karen Givens, 12; Laila Kazakevica, 13 (right); Lorraine Kourafas, 14; Maryellen Zwingle, 16; Sharon Morris, 13 (left); Stephanie Coffman, 6, 7 (right); Tan Kian Khoon, 29; Thomas Barrat, 22; Tyler Olson, 7 (left); Yan Simkin, 20; Zuzule, cover (American Paint)
UNICORN Stock Photos/Deneve Feigh Bunde, 15 (left); Dick Young, 17; Joel Dexter, 11

Capstone Press thanks Robert Coleman, PhD, associate professor, Equine Extension, Department of Animal Sciences at the University of Kentucky in Lexington for reviewing this book.